I0797695

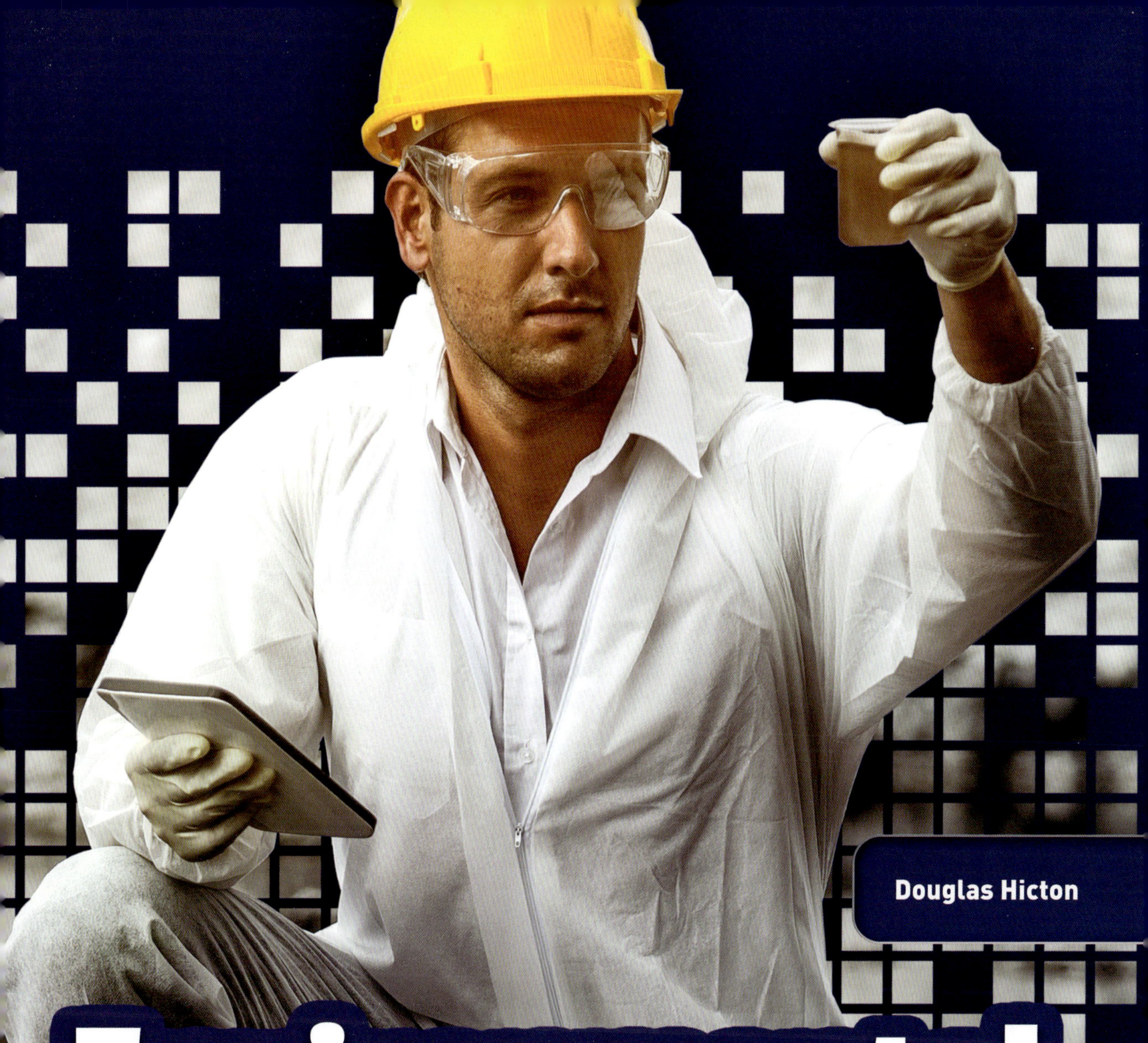

Douglas Hicton

Environmental Protection Agency

POWER • AUTHORITY • GOVERNANCE

LIGHTBOX
openlightbox.com

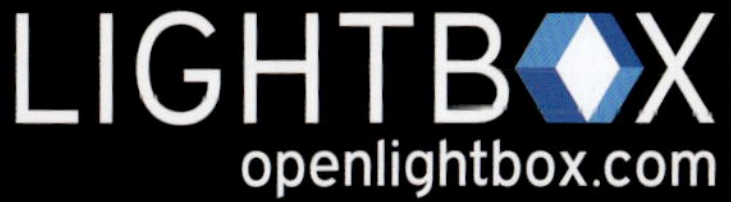

Go to **www.openlightbox.com** and enter this book's unique code.

ACCESS CODE

LBXF4579

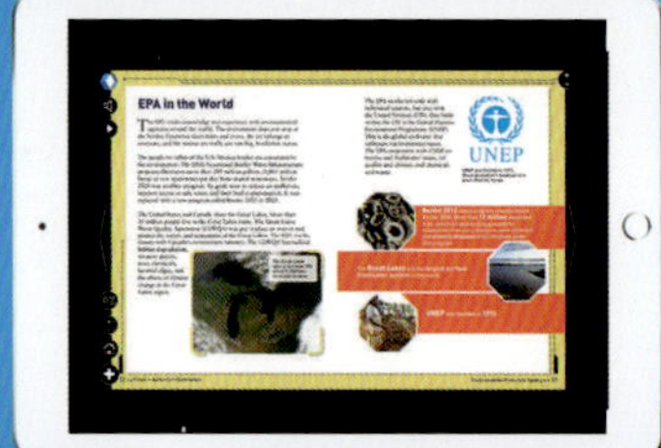

Lightbox is an all-inclusive digital solution for the teaching and learning of curriculum topics in an original, groundbreaking way. Lightbox is based on National Curriculum Standards.

LIGHTBOX SUPPLEMENTARY RESOURCES

SHARE
Share titles within your Learning Management System (LMS) or Library Circulation System

CURRICULUM
Find national and state curriculum correlations

CITATION
Create bibliographical references following APA, CMOS, and MLA styles

STANDARD FEATURES OF LIGHTBOX

AUDIO High-quality narration using text-to-speech system

ACTIVITIES Printable PDFs that can be emailed and graded

SLIDESHOWS Pictorial overviews of key concepts

VIDEOS Embedded high-definition video clips

WEBLINKS Curated links to external, child-safe resources

TRANSPARENCIES Step-by-step layering of maps, diagrams, charts, and timelines

INTERACTIVE MAPS Interactive maps and aerial satellite imagery

QUIZZES Ten multiple-choice questions that are automatically graded and emailed for teacher assessment

KEY WORDS Matching key concepts to their definitions

This title is part of our Lightbox digital subscription

Lightbox Grades 3–5 Subscription
ISBN 978-1-5105-5424-5

Access hundreds of Lightbox titles with our digital subscription. Sign up for a **FREE** subscription trial at **www.openlightbox.com/trial**

POWER • AUTHORITY • GOVERNANCE

Environmental Protection Agency

CONTENTS

Introduction

The environment consists of everything on Earth—land, water, air, plant life, and all the creatures that live on the planet, including people. This means that whatever harms the environment also harms human beings. The United States Environmental Protection Agency (EPA) is an independent agency of the federal government. It was formed to safeguard the environment in the United States. Since 1970, the agency has protected public health by setting limits on dangerous air **pollutants** that cause many serious diseases.

The EPA also helps provide clean water to Americans. It gives communities billions of dollars to improve their local water systems. Oil and chemical spills that damage coastal and inland waters are cleaned up under the supervision of the EPA as well.

The EPA's headquarters consists of several buildings in Washington, DC. They are in an area of the district known as the Federal Triangle.

The U.S. government's authority to create agencies such as the EPA comes from the people of the United States. As Thomas Jefferson wrote in the Declaration of Independence, government derives its powers from the consent of the governed. This idea is also known as "popular sovereignty." This means that the EPA acts in accordance with the will of the people of the United States.

In **1974**, the EPA created a **16-page booklet**, titled "**Fun With the Environment**," as a learning tool for children. More than **60 million copies** of it were distributed in cereal boxes.

The **EPA rates cars for fuel efficiency**. In **2020**, its **highest rating** among hybrid vehicles was for **59 miles per gallon**. (25 kilometers per liter)

Airborne lead concentrations in the United States **fell 98 percent** between **1980** and **2005**, after the EPA led the country to **phase out leaded gasoline**.

Origins of the EPA

In 1962, conservationist Rachel Carson published a book, *Silent Spring*, to raise public awareness of environmental pollution. Carson was a marine scientist and editor. She noticed that nearby forests had fallen silent. Birds no longer sang there because they had been wiped out by **pesticides** poisoning the food they ate.

At the time, every state had its own **regulations** to control pollution. However, some states were less strict than others, which affected neighboring states. Pollution travels with the wind and water. This means that **emissions** from sources such as smokestacks move downwind. Additionally, industrial chemicals dumped into one state's rivers affect life in states downstream.

On June 22, 1969, pollution in the Cuyahoga River in Cleveland, Ohio, burst into flames. However, this was not the first time, as the river had caught fire a dozen times before during the previous 100 years. The 1969 blaze is the best known, though, as Americans were becoming more aware of their environment during this time.

In response to this growing environmental crisis and confusing blend of different local environmental laws, President Richard M. Nixon created the EPA in late 1970. William D. Ruckelshaus became its first administrator. The EPA initially had the task of creating, monitoring, and enforcing national standards, as well as administering the Clean Air Act of 1970, which became law at the end of the year. The new agency took over some functions of three federal departments. These were Interior, Agriculture, and Health, Education, and Welfare.

One of the first actions taken by the newly-formed EPA in the early 1970s was to enact laws that led to the prosecution of companies responsible for polluting the Cuyahoga River.

Branches of Government

The EPA is an independent agency established by the **executive branch** of the U.S. government. The EPA administrator reports directly to the president of the United States. As the EPA is not a cabinet department, its administrator does not usually take part in cabinet meetings.

The EPA receives its funding from the annual federal budget passed by the Congress of the United States. The EPA can draft bills, such as the Clean Air Act or the Clean Water Act, but these do not become law until they are passed by both houses of Congress, the House of Representatives and the Senate, and signed by the president.

The U.S. government is organized so that no branch has unlimited authority. Not even the president has the last word. If the president chooses to **veto** a bill, Congress can override the veto. This is known as a system of "checks and balances."

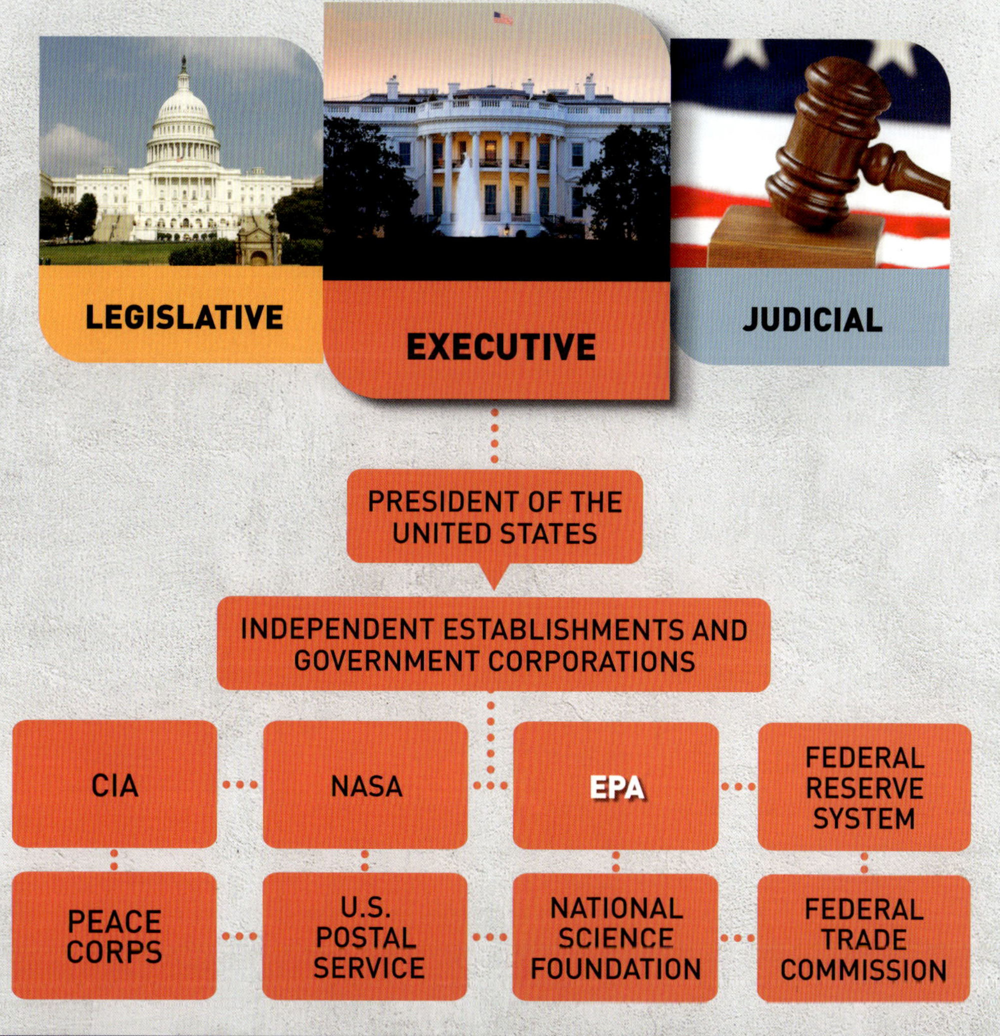

Purpose of the EPA

The mission of the EPA is clearly stated in its name. Congress writes environmental laws, and the EPA implements them through regulations. These laws and regulations promote the health and well-being of American citizens. The agency also decides on safe tolerance levels for pollutants in air, water, food, and even animal feed.

Regulations created by the EPA help clarify laws by adding details, such as the amount of a pollutant that is considered dangerous.

Although the EPA is a federal agency, it often works with other levels of government. For example, it provides grants to state and local environmental programs. Some of these are used for community cleanups of watcrways, toxic sites, and contaminated lands. The EPA also sometimes partners with businesses and **nonprofit** organizations. They share information and work together in many ways, including efforts to reduce **greenhouse gases**, lower pesticide usage, and conserve water and energy.

The EPA provides about $4 billion in grants to various groups and organizations every year. These help in many areas, such as wetland conservation.

One key power of the EPA is the ability to impose fines and other penalties on companies that violate national standards. Some standards may be enforced by states through their own regulations. Other standards are enforced by the EPA itself.

Fossil Fuels

In many parts of the United States, electricity is produced by coal-fired power plants. Coal is a **fossil fuel** that emits pollution, including greenhouse gases, sulfur dioxide, and soot. The EPA monitors these plants to ensure their emissions are acceptable. In 2000, the EPA told the Virginia Electric and Power Company (VEPCO) that it had violated the Clean Air Act. VEPCO had modified its largest facility, the Mount Storm power station in West Virginia, in a way that had greatly increased its emissions.

The EPA sued VEPCO and won. In 2003, the agency announced that the utility had agreed to eliminate 237,000 tons (215,000 metric tons) per year of sulfur dioxide and nitrogen oxides at eight of its plants in Virginia and West Virginia. It would cost VEPCO $1.2 billion over 10 years. This was the largest Clean Air Act settlement against a utility in EPA history.

EPA Through the Years

The EPA was created about half a century ago. Since then, it has sponsored a large amount of legislation to protect the environment. Today, the EPA continues to carry out its mission to keep Americans healthy.

September 27, 1962

Rachel Carson's *Silent Spring* is published. The book becomes a bestseller and jump-starts the environmental movement in the United States.

April 22, 1970

More than 20 million Americans, 10 percent of the U.S. population, take part in the first Earth Day. Twenty years later, Earth Day mobilizes 200 million people in 141 countries.

December 4, 1970

William D. Ruckelshaus is sworn in as the first EPA administrator. The EPA soon institutes a ban on DDT, the cancer-causing pesticide discussed in *Silent Spring*.

December 31, 1970

The Clean Air Act sets national air quality, auto emission, and anti-pollution standards in order to help improve health and reduce lead, sulfur dioxide, and other harmful pollutants.

October 18, 1972

The Clean Water Act is passed by Congress. Its purpose is to prevent pollution, assist wastewater treatment facilities, and maintain and restore American waters and wetlands.

August 7, 1978

President Jimmy Carter declares a state of emergency at the Love Canal in Niagara Falls, New York. Toxic waste forces the evacuation of 239 families living in the area.

May 24, 1982

The EPA requires all U.S. schools to test their buildings for asbestos, an insulation material that can cause cancer in human beings.

November 18, 1988

President Ronald Reagan signs the Ocean Dumping Ban Act into law. It prohibits all municipal and industrial waste dumping into the ocean after December 31, 1991.

January 1, 1996

The EPA phases out leaded gasoline in vehicles. This causes blood levels of lead in U.S. children to drop 70 percent from those in 1970. Lead poisoning can damage the central nervous system and cause slowed growth.

September 11, 2001

Terrorists attack and destroy the World Trade Center in New York City. The EPA tests air, water, and dust for possible environmental hazards at the site of the attack. The organization also helps clear toxic materials away from the area.

August 29, 2005

Hurricane Katrina devastates the Gulf Coast, breaching levees in southeast Louisiana. Soon, seawater floods 80 percent of New Orleans. The EPA works with other federal and state agencies to assess damage from the disaster.

October 12, 2007

The Nobel Peace Prize is shared by former vice president Al Gore and the Intergovernmental Panel on Climate Change (IPCC). Thirty of the IPCC scientists are EPA employees.

January 23, 2009

Lisa P. Jackson becomes the first African American EPA administrator.

January 20, 2021

President Joe Biden signs an order instructing the United States to rejoin the Paris Climate Accord limiting greenhouse gas emissions.

EPA Issues

The EPA is intended to act in a neutral fashion. Its job is to keep the air people breathe from smothering them, and the food and water they consume from poisoning them. However, the amount of power that the EPA has, along with the effects that its actions can have on people, businesses, and governments, has made the organization itself the subject of controversy.

The EPA answers directly to the president of the United States. Some presidents have favored stronger environmental regulations. Others have felt that these regulations are too strict and have sought to weaken or abolish them. This means that the EPA's priorities can change when the president changes.

People may also oppose the EPA for other reasons. To many Americans, the organization represents federal **overreach** and **bureaucratic** waste. Others argue that the United States should not have national standards. They would rather have the states take full responsibility for managing their own environments.

In 2022, the U.S. federal government restored rules requiring projects such as highways and oil wells to undergo strict environmental reviews. These had been struck down during the previous administration.

Other concerns relating to the EPA are economic in nature. Individuals and corporations may feel that EPA regulations increase business costs beyond what is reasonable. This means that, in order to stay profitable, businesses must then pass the costs along to consumers. Otherwise, if they do not raise their prices, they may go out of business, causing workers to lose their jobs.

Emergency Planning and Community Right-to-Know Act (EPCRA)

In 1984, a pesticide plant owned by American company Union Carbide accidentally released a lethal gas into the air near Bhopal, India. The gas killed thousands of people and injured thousands more. No one had been prepared for a disaster of this kind.

Americans were worried about a similar catastrophe happening in the United States. Congress passed the EPCRA Act in 1986, to be implemented by EPA. It requires companies to report chemical releases to the correct authorities. The authorities in turn make this information publicly available.

Governments may fine facilities up to $75,000 per day if they do not comply with EPCRA provisions. Citizens can also sue a facility, their state's emergency response commission, their governor, or the EPA for not providing information that must be made public under EPCRA. Anyone who knowingly withholds this information can receive a fine of up to $50,000 or five years in prison.

The chemical released in the 1984 Bhopal disaster was called methyl isocyanate. It is used in the production of pesticides.

Key Figures in the EPA

The EPA is responsible for protecting the environment throughout the nation. Key figures throughout the EPA's history have served the United States in many ways.

William D. Ruckelshaus

William D. Ruckelshaus (1932–2019) was the first EPA administrator. In 1973, he left to serve as acting FBI director, and then Deputy Attorney General. In 1983, Ruckelshaus returned to the EPA as its administrator. He was the only person to lead the EPA twice.

Carol M. Browner

Carol M. Browner (1955–) was the longest-serving EPA administrator, leading it from 1993 to 2001. Browner oversaw the first major restoration plan for the **Everglades**. She also gave priority to the cleanup of "brownfields," contaminated industrial sites and urban properties.

Christine Todd Whitman

Christine Todd Whitman (1946–) became the EPA's administrator in 2001. In this role, she oversaw the cleanup of New York's Hudson River. Whitman also introduced the Clear Skies Initiative, a mandatory program intended to reduce power plant emissions.

Love Canal

HISTORICAL CASE STUDY

Starting in the 1920s, Niagara Falls, New York, had been using an area known as Love Canal as a dump. Hooker Chemical Company, which took over the 70-acre (28-hectare) property, also dumped chemicals there from about 1942 to 1952. In 1953, Hooker sold the area back to the city for one dollar. Soon, roads were laid, utility lines were buried, and homes were constructed. The city built an elementary school, park, and baseball field.

However, by 1970, many residents had developed suspicious health problems. Pools of chemicals began to appear. In 1976, after three years of record rainfall, toxic waste began to leach into backyards, basements, and the school. Children came home from the playground with burned hands and faces.

The EPA, New York state, and Niagara county began doing tests in the area. The EPA tests found 82 different chemicals, including highly dangerous dioxin. In 1978, President Carter declared Love Canal a federal health emergency. The Justice department sued Hooker for more than $117 million on behalf of the EPA. A massive cleanup of the area cost $400 million. Parts of Love Canal are still considered unsafe today.

In total, about 22,000 tons (20,000 metric tons) of chemicals were dumped in Love Canal.

Careers in the EPA

Climate Change Analyst

A climate change analyst's job has two parts. The scientific part of the job includes climate research and analyzing raw data from scientists. The political side of the job involves using the data to help create laws and policies. This career is recommended for people who care deeply about climate issues.

Industrial Ecologist

Curious types make good industrial ecologists. An ecologist may investigate a chemical spill inside a manufacturing plant one day. The next day may be spent outdoors testing the water quality of a river or lake. As ecologists are on their feet most of the time, this job can be physically demanding.

Environmental Restoration Planner

Environmental restoration planners conduct laboratory and field tests. They often work on teams with scientists, engineers, and technicians in other fields. Planners monitor the environment and investigate sources of pollution. Some also inspect public places and businesses for hazards.

Hydrologist

Hydrologists study water and the water cycle. They often work in the field, collecting samples or inspecting pollution-monitoring equipment. In the lab, many hydrologists use computer models to forecast future water supplies and the spread of pollution. Some hydrologists work with policymakers to develop conservation plans.

The **EPA's 2020 budget** was about **$9.1 billion**. Almost **half** of this went into grants to state environmental programs, charities, and educational institutions.

The **top salary** of an **EPA environmental engineer** is more than **$140,000** per year.

Since **2004, EPA scientists** and engineers have **shared their knowledge** with local students through the **STEM Outreach program**. Today, they have volunteered more than **19,000 hours of time**.

Tools of the Trade

The EPA requires many different types of tools and devices to do its job. Some are used to find impurities and pollutants in water, air, and soil. Others are for calibrating the massive amounts of data the EPA collects.

Radiation Detectors

Radiation detectors are used in places where there has been a nuclear accident. These events can cause dangerous levels of radiation, presenting a severe threat for EPA workers. Radiation detectors tell scientists if an area is safe for humans and, if unsafe, can let them know what amount of protection is needed.

Particulate Matter Sensors

Coal-burning factories, wildfires, and cars all produce smoke, which contains carbon monoxide, carbon dioxide, and soot particles. Soot hangs in the air because its particles are very small and light. If people breathe these particles in, they can be dangerous. EPA scientists use particulate matter sensors to find out if a community's air is contaminated.

TAGA

The Trace Atmospheric Gas Analyzer (TAGA) can be used to find compounds in the air at otherwise undetectable levels. Its specialized equipment can sample and analyze in real time. As the TAGA is mobile, it allows scientists to measure air quality at remote locations. The EPA uses TAGA in disaster areas to identify threats quickly.

Satellites

Satellites can be used both for communications and to track weather events such as tornadoes and hurricanes. Today, the EPA is also working with other government agencies to track pollution with satellites. Satellite images change from day to day, showing where the pollution has been. This makes it easier to figure out how it is moving.

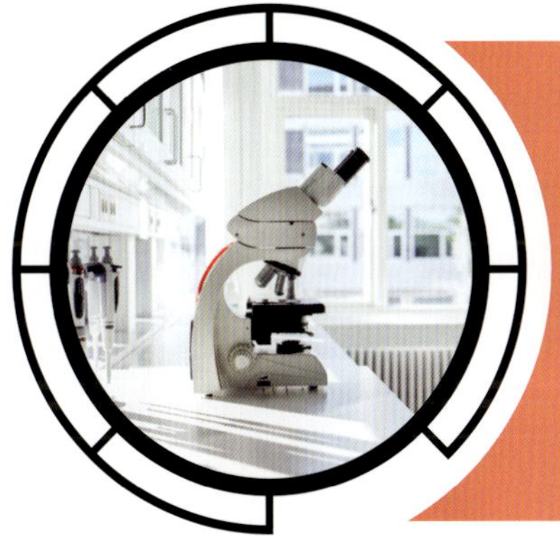

Microscopes

In order to detect microscopic, highly **contagious** parasites, EPA workers go into communities to collect soil and water samples. They take these samples back to the lab and examine them under microscopes. These tools magnify samples, allowing people to see tiny objects. If they see parasites, the EPA can issue a warning.

PPE

EPA responders have been wearing personal protective equipment (PPE) for years. Some areas are so polluted that EPA staff would be at risk if they did not wear PPE. The PPE for extremely hazardous situations includes totally **encapsulated** chemical- and vapor-protective suits. The PPE worn in less hazardous situations includes gloves, coveralls, and safety glasses.

EPA in the United States

The EPA works across the United States. It has 10 regional offices spread throughout the country. The EPA also responds to accidents around the nation.

1

Hanford Site, Washington

The Hanford Site nuclear production facility contains storage tanks holding 56 million gallons (212 million L) of radioactive toxic waste. Tanks have been leaking since at least 2010, causing waste to leach into the water system and soil. The EPA set guidelines for reclaiming the land. Cleanup is still going on today.

Hawaii

2

SCALE

250 KILOMETERS

100 MILES

2

Kamilo Beach, Hawaii

The white sands of Kamilo Beach are covered with garbage. The beach, near the south tip of the Big Island, has been nicknamed "Plastic Beach." In 2020, environmental groups sued the EPA to make the state solve the trash problem. The groups won, and the EPA instructed Hawaii to clean up Kamilo.

3
Flint, Michigan
Michigan's state government changed the source of Flint's water supply to the Flint River in 2014. Tests by the EPA and other organizations in 2015 showed dangerous levels of lead in the water. Later that year, the EPA formed a Flint Safe Drinking Water Task Force to help with the situation.
New Hampshire
Vermont
Maine
Massachusetts
Rhode Island
Connecticut
New Jersey
Delaware
Maryland
District of Columbia
North Dakota
Minnesota
South Dakota
Wisconsin
Michigan
New York
Pennsylvania
Iowa
Nebraska
Illinois
Indiana
Ohio
West Virginia
Virginia
Kansas
Missouri
Kentucky
North Carolina
Tennessee
South Carolina
Oklahoma
Arkansas
Alabama
Georgia
Mississippi
Texas
Louisiana
Florida
Atlantic Ocean
Gulf of Mexico
N
W
E
S
4
Middletown, Pennsylvania
On March 28, 1979, the Three Mile Island Unit 2 reactor partly melted down. It was the most serious commercial nuclear power plant accident in U.S. history. Within hours, the EPA's Office of Radiation Programs began taking daily samples near the damaged reactor. The agency then expanded outward to monitor 31 power stations within a 7-mile (11-km) radius.

EPA in the World

The EPA trades knowledge and experience with environmental agencies around the world. The environment does not stop at the border. Countries share lakes and rivers, the air belongs to everyone, and the oceans are really just one big, borderless ocean.

The people on either side of the U.S.-Mexico border are connected by the environment. The EPA's bi-national Border Water **Infrastructure** program eliminates more than 280 million gallons (1,060 million L) of raw wastewater per day from shared waterways. Border 2020 was another program that promoted cooperation between the two nations. Its goals were to reduce air pollution, improve access to safe water, and limit land contamination. It was replaced with an updated program called Border 2025 in 2021.

The United States and Canada share the Great Lakes. More than 30 million people live in the Great Lakes basin. The Great Lakes Water Quality Agreement (GLWQA) was put in place to restore and protect the waters and **ecosystems** of the Great Lakes. As part of the agreement between the two countries, the EPA works closely with Canada's environment ministry. The GLWQA has tackled **habitat degradation**, invasive species, toxic chemicals, harmful algae, and the effects of climate change in the Great Lakes region.

The Great Lakes span more than 750 miles (1,200 km) from east to west.

The EPA works not only with individual nations, but also with the United Nations (UN). One body within the UN is the United Nations Environment Programme (UNEP). This is the global authority that addresses environmental issues. The EPA cooperates with UNEP on marine and freshwater issues, air quality and climate, and chemicals and waste.

UNEP's headquarters are located in Nairobi, Kenya.

Border 2012 was a program enacted before **Border 2020**. More than **12 million** discarded tires, which act as breeding grounds for mosquitoes that carry diseases, were collected and **properly disposed** of by initiatives under this program.

The **Great Lakes** are the **largest surface freshwater system** in the world.

UNEP was founded in **1972**.

EPA Today

For 50 years, EPA researchers have been **innovators** in environmental science. They have created new tools to make their work more efficient, timely, and accurate. New methods have replaced old ones. The innovation has all served the purpose of protecting the environment and the health of the people of the United States.

One major problem facing the EPA in recent years is the COVID-19 pandemic, which began in 2019. EPA researchers are working with the Centers for Disease Control and Prevention (CDC) on new ways to measure levels of the virus that causes COVID-19 in wastewater. Not everyone exposed to the virus shows symptoms, but water that goes down their drains and toilets can contain the virus. Higher levels in an area may mean an outbreak will occur there soon. Health officials can tell the public where these viral hot spots are, helping people to take extra care.

The EPA works to combat disinformation relating to diseases. For example, in 2021, the agency updated rules preventing companies from making false claims about the ability of disinfectants to protect surfaces from viruses. EPA scientists are also studying more effective ways to disinfect large spaces with **antimicrobial** products, as well as new methods of disinfecting PPE.

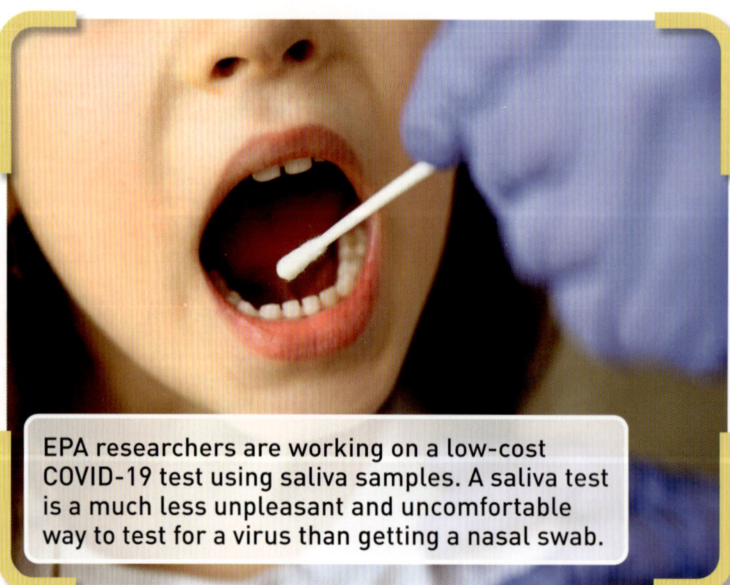

EPA researchers are working on a low-cost COVID-19 test using saliva samples. A saliva test is a much less unpleasant and uncomfortable way to test for a virus than getting a nasal swab.

Deepwater Horizon

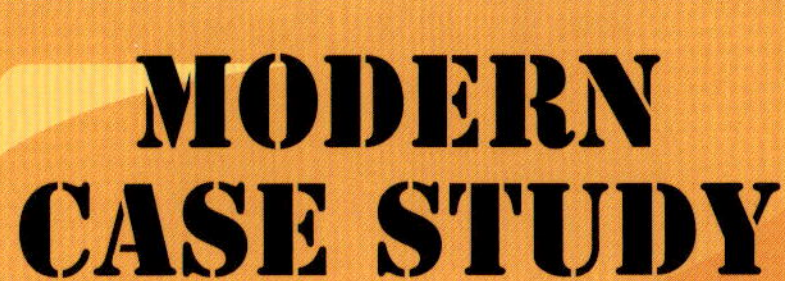

On April 20, 2010, the offshore oil rig *Deepwater Horizon* blew up and sank in the Gulf of Mexico. Millions of barrels of oil gushed out of the well for 87 days. Sticky, black crude covered beaches from Louisiana to Florida.

It was the worst marine spill in U.S. history. Countless sea creatures died. More than 10 years later, many species still struggle with low numbers, while a few others have rebounded. The Gulf Coast fishing industry was devastated as many fishers lost their livelihood. The U.S. government took British Petroleum (BP), which owned the rig, to court. Among other legal settlements, the company paid $9.2 billion as part of a class action lawsuit, while also paying for the cleanup.

The EPA provided support for the cleanup effort. EPA fieldworkers collected onshore samples of chemicals that had been sprayed into the water to disperse the oil. They monitored the effects of those dispersants in the air, water, and sediment. EPA scientists also collected and studied masses of information, which was shared with other agencies.

BP was found guilty of 11 counts of manslaughter, obstruction of Congress, and violating the Clean Water Act.

The *Deepwater Horizon* blast killed 11 workers from BP.

EPA Looking to the Future

The United States faces some special challenges. Much of the country was caught off guard by COVID-19. It has reshaped the economy and produced high rates of unemployment. It has also led to instances of unrest and turmoil.

In addition, the problem of climate change, largely caused by fossil-fuel emissions, remains. Scientists hold climate change responsible for drastic changes in the environment. Ice caps melt, habitats are destroyed, and species are lost. Most climate scientists say that Earth has until 2030 before many of these changes are irreversible. Today, some parts of the country already experience severe weather conditions. These include droughts, floods, extreme heat, wildfires, and a longer hurricane season.

The 2021 hurricane season was one of the most expensive on record. Hurricane Ida, which struck Louisiana, caused more than $64.5 billion worth of damage.

Looking to the future, the EPA has several tools beyond the creation of new regulations that it can use to address these challenges. One major goal is to improve public education about environmental issues. Another is securing partnerships, allowing the organization to work alongside businesses and charities to help protect the environment more effectively. These steps will be essential in helping the EPA address both ongoing and new environmental issues in the coming years.

The EPA is taking steps to improve access to clean water across the country. The agency's goal is to increase the amount of watersheds that meet its standards by 41,000 square miles (106,000 sq. km) by 2026.

One long-term goal for the EPA is to reduce the amount of hydrochlorofluorocarbons released by industries into the atmosphere. These chemicals, often used in liquid or gas form for refrigeration, can damage the ozone layer if they enter Earth's atmosphere.

ACTIVITY ★★

Create a Policy Paper

Hydraulic fracturing, or fracking, is a way to recover natural gas from shale rock. It is done by drilling down to the shale and pumping in a large volume of high-pressure water, mixed with chemicals and sand. This fractures the shale, and the released gas is pumped out. The EPA says it is possible that fracking liquid may seep into aquifers that supply drinking water.

Some environmental activists want the government to ban the practice. They claim fracking has caused earthquakes in Oklahoma and that it releases too many greenhouse gases. However, the United States Geological Survey (USGS) reports that only 2 percent of earthquakes result from fracking.

Develop your own thoughts about whether hydraulic fracturing should continue in the United States. Write a policy paper that summarizes your opinions.

Step 1:

Answer the following questions to help you develop your opinions.

1. Do you think fracking should be banned? Why or why not?
2. Are some greenhouse gas emissions an acceptable price to pay for cheap, abundant energy? Why or why not?
3. Some arguments for fracking say it creates important jobs for people right now. Others argue that it could pollute local water systems with toxic chemicals, which may have long-term consequences. Are both arguments valid? Why or why not?
4. Activists say fracking causes earthquakes. However, the United States Geological Survey (USGS) says its effect is very small. Which argument do you think is stronger? Why?

5. What would determine the trustworthiness of the source of one of the arguments from questions 3 or 4? Why?
6. How might natural gas compare to other forms of fossil fuels in terms of environmental impact? Does this make it a resource worth using? Why or why not?
7. How might natural gas compare to renewable forms of energy? What are the pros and cons of each?

Step 2:

Take your opinions from questions 1 to 7 and write a one-page policy paper. This should explain whether fracking is a practice that should be expanded, kept the same, or reduced. Follow the format outlined below.

- Paragraph 1: What is the question you are addressing?
- Paragraph 2: What are the issues surrounding the question?
- Paragraph 3: What is your policy on the issue, and why?

QUIZ ★★

1 Who was the only person to serve as administrator of the EPA twice?

2 What is the purpose of the Clean Air Act?

3 Which oil company owned the oil rig *Deepwater Horizon*?

4 What is TAGA?

5 Who wrote *Silent Spring*, and in which year was it published?

6 Which two countries signed the GLWQA?

7 Which U.S. president created the EPA?

8 What Hawaiian beach has been nicknamed "Plastic Beach"?

9 Which president declared Love Canal a federal health emergency?

10 To which branch of the U.S. government does the EPA belong?

ANSWERS

1. William D. Ruckelshaus 2. To set national air quality, auto emission, and anti-pollution standards 3. British Petroleum 4. A mobile tool for monitoring air quality 5. Rachel Carson, in 1962 6. Canada and the United States 7. Richard M. Nixon 8. Kamilo Beach 9. Jimmy Carter 10. Executive branch

KEY WORDS ★★

antimicrobial: germ-killing

bureaucratic: relating to a system for controlling or managing a country

contagious: spreading from one person or organism to another

ecosystems: organisms interacting with each other and their local environment

emissions: gases and smoke discharged into the air by factories or by gasoline-powered vehicles

encapsulated: fully enclosed and self-contained so nothing harmful can enter

Everglades: a large wetland area found in southern Florida

executive branch: the U.S. president, vice president, and cabinet

fossil fuel: coal, oil, gasoline, or natural gas

greenhouse gases: gases that trap the Sun's heat in the atmosphere

habitat degradation: when a natural habitat is changed so much that it no longer supports the species it originally sustained

infrastructure: basic facilities that support modern human life

innovators: people who introduce new ideas, products, or methods

nonprofit: a public charitable organization set up to benefit the public instead of for profit

overreach: going beyond what one should do

pesticides: chemicals used for killing insects or other organisms harmful to cultivated plants or animals

pollutants: harmful substances that contaminate the air or water

regulations: rules set up by governments that outline how something is to be done

veto: the power of a president to forbid a piece of legislation

INDEX ★★

LIGHTBOX

SUPPLEMENTARY RESOURCES

Click on the plus icon found in the bottom left corner of each spread to open additional teacher resources.

- Download and print the book's quizzes and activities
- Access curriculum correlations
- Explore additional web applications that enhance the Lightbox experience

LIGHTBOX DIGITAL TITLES
Packed full of integrated media

VIDEOS

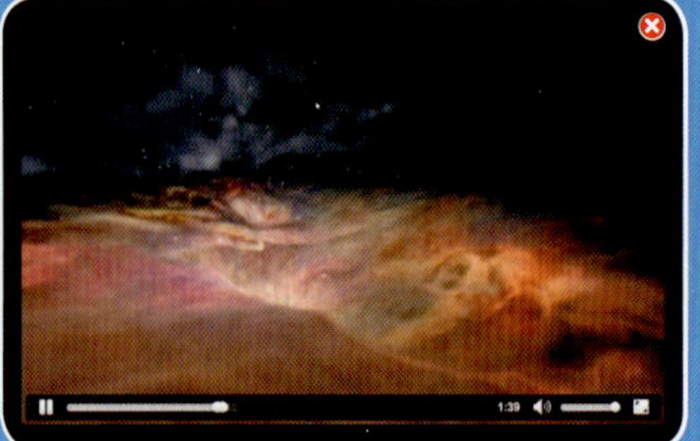

INTERACTIVE MAPS

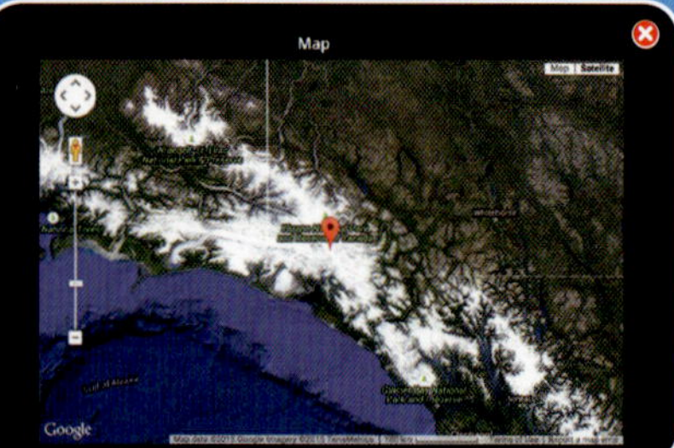

WEBLINKS

SLIDESHOWS

QUIZZES

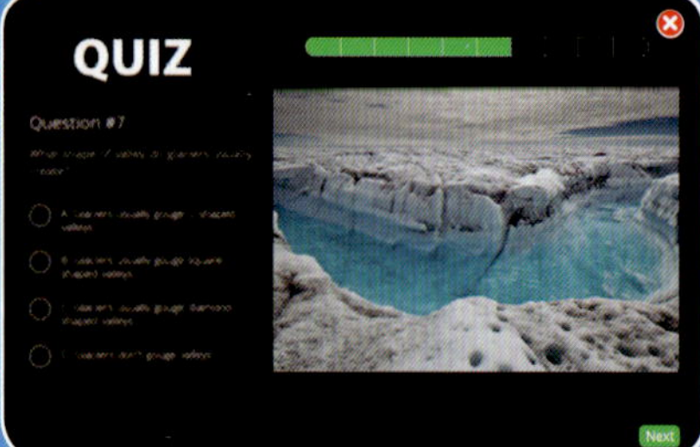

OPTIMIZED FOR
- ✓ TABLETS
- ✓ SMARTBOARDS
- ✓ COMPUTERS
- ✓ AND MUCH MORE!

Published by Lightbox Learning Inc.
276 5th Avenue, Suite 704 #917
New York, NY 10001
Website: www.openlightbox.com

Library of Congress Cataloging-in-Publication Data
Names: Hicton, Douglas, author.
Title: Environmental Protection Agency / Douglas Hicton.
Description: New York : Lightbox, 2021. | Series: Power, authority, and governance | Includes index. | Audience: Grades 4-6
Identifiers: LCCN 2021033730 (print) | LCCN 2021033731 (ebook) | ISBN 9781510558878 (library binding) | ISBN 9781510558885
Subjects: LCSH: United States. Environmental Protection Agency--Juvenile literature. | Environmental law--United States--Juvenile literature. | Environmental policy--United States--Juvenile literature.
Classification: LCC KF3817.4 . H53 2021 (print) | LCC KF3817.4 (ebook) | DDC 363.700973--dc23
LC record available at https://lccn.loc.gov/2021033730
LC ebook record available at https://lccn.loc.gov/2021033731

Printed in Guangzhou, China
1 2 3 4 5 6 7 8 9 0 27 26 25 24 23

012023
111121

Art Director: Terry Paulhus Project Coordinator: John Willis

Every reasonable effort has been made to trace ownership and to obtain permission to reprint copyright material. The publisher would be pleased to have any errors or omissions brought to its attention so that they may be corrected in subsequent printings.

The publisher acknowledges Alamy, the EPA, Getty Images, Shutterstock, and Wikimedia as the primary image suppliers for this title.